Earthquakes

Michele Ingber Drohan

The Rosen Publishing Group's
PowerKids Press™
New York

For Dawn, who was with me when the earth shook.

Published in 1999 by The Rosen Publishing Group, Inc.
29 East 21st Street, New York, NY 10010

First Edition

Book Design: Danielle Primiceri

Photo Credits: Cover, p. 6 © 1996 Andromeda Interactive Ltd, Corbis-Bettman; p. 9 © Elliott Smith/International Stock; p. 10 © Philip Wallick/FPG International; p. 13 © Frank Grant/International Stock; p. 14 © 1990 Warren Faidley/International Stock; p. 17 © Bartruff, David/FPG International; p. 18 © Seth Dinnerman; p. 21 © Scott Thode/International Stock; p. 22 © 1988 Dario Perla/International Stock.

Drohan, Michele Ingber.
    Earthquakes / by Michele Ingber Drohan.
        p.   cm.— (Natural disasters)
    Includes index.
    Summary: Explains what earthquakes are, why they happen, how they are studied and how to protect yourself in an earthquake.
    ISBN 0-8239-5285-1
    1. Earthquakes—Juvenile literature. [1. Earthquakes.] I. Title. II. Series: Drohan, Michele Ingber. Natural disasters.
QE521.3.D75 1998
551.22—dc21
                                           97-39480
                                           CIP
                                         AC

Manufactured in the United States of America

Contents

Earth

Earth is made up of three layers of rock. The center of Earth is called the core. The inner core is solid rock. The outer core is hot, liquid rock. The middle section is called the **mantle** (MAN-tul). The mantle is solid rock with pockets of liquid rock inside it. The outer section is called the crust. The crust is made of solid rock and it covers the whole surface of Earth. The crust is broken up into about twenty pieces called plates.

It's hard to believe, but 250 million years ago, all of these plates were joined together. They formed one huge **continent** (KON-tih-nent) called **Pangaea** (pan-GEE-uh).

The crust is the thinnest of Earth's layers. We live on the crust. ▶

CRUST

CORE

MANTLE

North America

South America

Alfred Wegener

Plate Tectonics

In 1915 a scientist named Alfred Wegener discovered African plant **fossils** (FOS-sulz) in South America. He thought this was strange because Africa and South America are so far apart. Then he noticed that when he looked at a map, it seemed as if the different continents could fit together. He called this idea **plate tectonics** (PLAYT tek-TAH-niks). This means that the plates in Earth's crust can move.

It has taken millions of years for these plates to move to where they are now. And they are still moving today. But you can't feel the ground moving because the plates move very slowly.

◄ *Look closely at the coastlines of Africa and South America. Can you see how they could have fit together at one tme?*

How an Earthquake Happens

When one plate runs into another plate it can cause trouble in Earth's crust. The plates push against each other but have nowhere to go. The place where this happens is called a **fault line** (FAWLT LYN). The power of the moving plates causes a lot of **pressure** (PRESH-er).

As the plates continue to push against each other over many years, pressure builds and builds. When the pressure builds up too much, the plates suddenly move. All that pressure is let go. This sends **shock waves** (SHOK WAYVZ) through Earth's crust. The shock waves make the ground shake and tremble. This is called an earthquake.

Earthquakes often cause large cracks to form in the ground, such as this one in California. ▶

The San Andreas Fault

The San Andreas Fault is the most famous fault line in the United States. It runs all the way down the California coastline. It is the place where the North American plate and the Pacific plate meet.

The city of San Francisco is on the North American plate. The city of Los Angeles is on the Pacific plate. Right now the cities are about 400 miles apart. But as the plates move in opposite directions, the cities get closer. Scientists say that one day Los Angeles and San Francisco will be neighbors! This fault line has been the place of many earthquakes. In fact, one of the biggest earthquakes in United States history happened in San Francisco in 1906.

◄ *The San Andreas Fault has been the cause of at least one major earthquake per year from 1988 to 1997.*

WING LUKE ELEMENTARY

Seismologists

Did you know that earthquakes happen every day all over the world? Most are so small that nobody feels them. But we know they happen because **seismologists** (syz-MAH-luh-jists) study movement in Earth's crust. Shock waves in the crust are recorded by a **seismograph** (SYZ-muh-graf).

Every time Earth's crust moves it causes a needle on the seismograph to move. This needle draws a line on paper every time it moves. When the needle makes a long line, it means the movement is very strong. The seismologists can also find the exact point inside Earth where an earthquake struck. This is called the **epicenter** (EP-ih-SEN-ter).

This seismologist studies fault lines even if they are buried under snow and ice. ▶

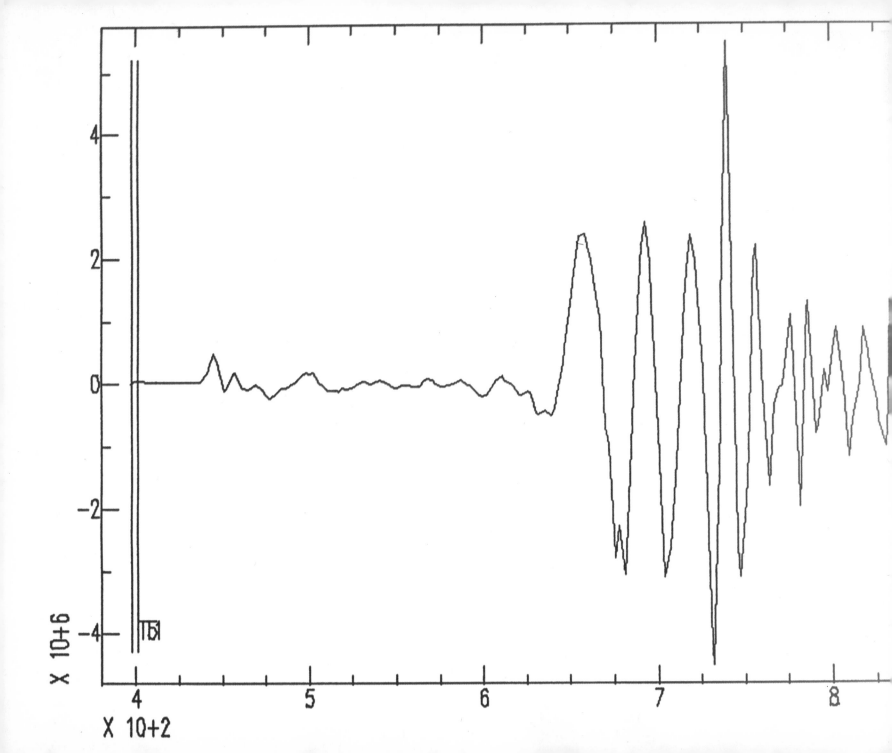

Measuring Earthquakes

Seismologists use two scales to measure earthquakes. One is the **Richter Scale** (RIK-ter SKAYL). It measures how strong an earthquake is. If the seismograph shows a lot of movement, an earthquake gets a high number. A ten is the highest number on the Richter Scale. The highest number ever to be measured by the Richter Scale was 8.4, in Anchorage, Alaska, in 1964.

The **Mercalli Scale** (mer-KAL-lee SKAYL) measures how badly an earthquake **damages** (DAM-ih-jiz) an area. The higher the number on the scale, the more damage done. Even when an earthquake is strong, if it happens in a place with few buildings and people, the number on the Mercalli Scale will be low.

◄ *The tallest line on this seismograph reading shows the Loma Prieta earthquake that happened on October 17, 1989.*

Destruction

On January 17, 1994, at 4:30 in the morning, a big earthquake hit Los Angeles, California. People woke up to a loud rumble. The ground shook for 45 seconds. Highways broke apart. Buildings crumbled and some caught fire. The earthquake meaured 6.7 on the Richter Scale. Sixty people died. Many people had no electric power or water for days. **Aftershocks** (AF-ter-shoks) lasted for months. It took many weeks for the city to recover. The people of the city worked hard to repair the damage and help others get food, water, and shelter.

The highways in California are often in danger of ▶
collapsing because of earthquakes.

Protect Yourself!

The biggest danger during an earthquake is from falling objects. If you ever experience an earthquake, you can protect yourself from getting hurt.

If you feel an earthquake and you're inside
* stay away from windows and
* get in a doorway or under a big desk or table.

If you're outside
* move away from power lines and telephone poles,
* stay away from tall buildings, and move to an open area.

The most important thing is to try to stay calm and remember that you'll be okay.

Practicing what you'll do if there's an earthquake is a good way to prepare you and your family for when there is a real emergency.

19

Building Better Buildings

Many city planners have learned from the work of seismologists. They are trying to build buildings that will stand up to an earthquake. This means building with **flexible** (FLEK-sih-bul) materials. These materials, such as rubber and steel, let a building bend or sway when Earth moves. Buildings made from materials that aren't flexible can fall apart from the shock of an earthquake.

Along with making buildings stronger, many cities try to protect the people of the city in other ways. Some cities have teams of people who help those who have been in a disaster. When people act quickly, it is easier to find and help those who are hurt.

Many of the older buildings in the city of San Francisco have been rebuilt with new, flexible materials so they won't collapse, as this building did. ▶

Predicting Earthquakes

Seismologists have not found a way to **predict** (pre-DIKT) earthquakes. Even with special instruments, nobody can say exactly *when* an earthquake will happen.

But seismologists do know *where* they might happen. They study fault lines. They know that a fault line that hasn't had an earthquake in a while may have one soon. This is because pressure has been building up. It's just a matter of time before the pressure is let go. By studying earthquakes, seismologists hope to learn better ways to protect people and their homes from the danger of earthquakes.

Web Sites:

You can learn more about earthquakes at this Web site: http://www.fema.gov/kids/

Glossary

aftershock (AF-ter-shok) A tremble in Earth's crust in the days, weeks, and months after an earthquake.

continent (KON-tih-nent) One of seven main pieces of land on Earth.

damage (DAM-ij) To cause harm.

epicenter (EP-ih-SEN-ter) The place on Earth's surface where an earthquake happens.

fault line (FAVVLT LYN) The place on Earth's surface where two plates meet.

flexible (FLEK-sih-bul) Being able to move and bend in different ways.

fossil (FOS-sul) The remains of a plant or animal from long ago that are buried in Earth's crust.

mantle (MAN-tul) The middle layer of Earth.

Mercalli Scale (mer-KAL-lee SKAYL) An instrument that measures the damage caused by an earthquake.

Pangaea (pan-GEE-uh) The name of the one piece of land that scientists believe broke into the seven continents millions of years ago.

plate tectonics (PLAYT tek-TAH-niks) The idea that the plates in Earth's crust move.

predict (pre-DIKT) To know something is going to happen before it happens.

pressure (PRESH-er) A force put on something.

Richter Scale (RIK-ter SKAYL) An instrument that measures how strong an earthquake is.

seismograph (SYZ-muh-graf) An instrument that measures movement in Earth's crust.

seismologist (syz-MAH-luh-jist) A person who studies earthquakes.

shock wave (SHOK WAYV) A big, sudden burst of energy that comes from the rocks in Earth's crust.

Index